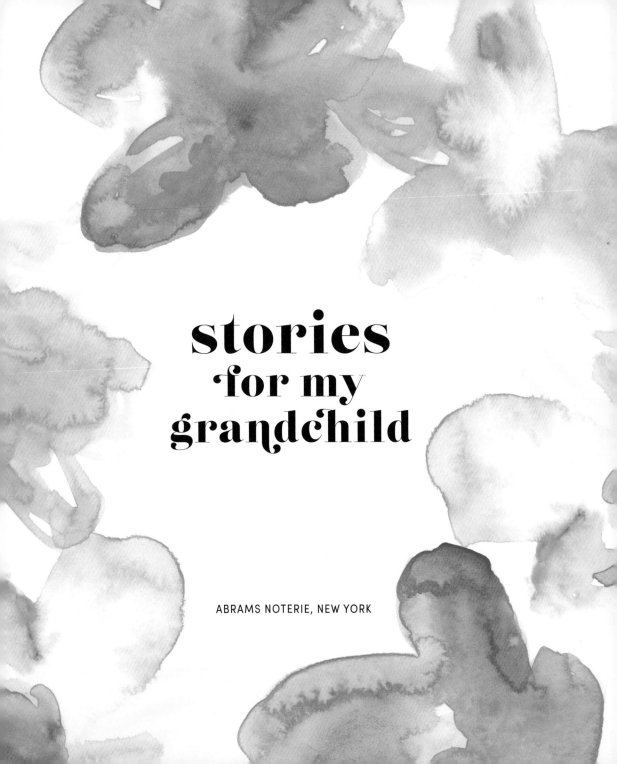

stories
for my
grandchild

ABRAMS NOTERIE, NEW YORK

dear friends,

I DON'T KNOW YOUR NAMES, BUT I DO KNOW WHO YOU ARE.
YOU ARE GRANDMA, GIGI, NONNA, YAYA, MIMI, ABUELITA, GEEMA, MEME,
OR, IN MY CASE, HONEY.

You are a giver of kisses, a provider of treats, and a source of unconditional love and solace. You are a grandmother, and your grandchildren know exactly what to call you. *But, do they know who you are?*

I have always said that the greatest gifts we leave our grandchildren are the lessons we share, the adventures we catalog, and the love we shower. It is my heartfelt pleasure to present you with this journal to record your own treasured stories, family history, and personal vignettes.

Sharing stories from your past gives your grandchildren a sense of identity, a connection to their heritage, and a deeper relationship with you. Your grandchildren will love knowing what you excelled at in elementary school, what dating was like when you were a teenager, and how you embraced opportunities or faced challenges throughout adulthood.

I am Honey Good, a wife, mother, grandmother to twenty-five grandchildren, and founder of HoneyGood.com. My website is devoted to encouraging women over fifty to be visible, vibrant, and inspiring to the next generation. I know who you are, because we belong to the same sorority: grandmotherhood!

With the gift of this journal, your grandchildren will know you for more than kisses and comfort. They will learn about their family through your stories and, more importantly, about the values that they will hand down to future generations.

I AM SMILING,

The greatest gift we give our grandchildren is what we leave in their heads.

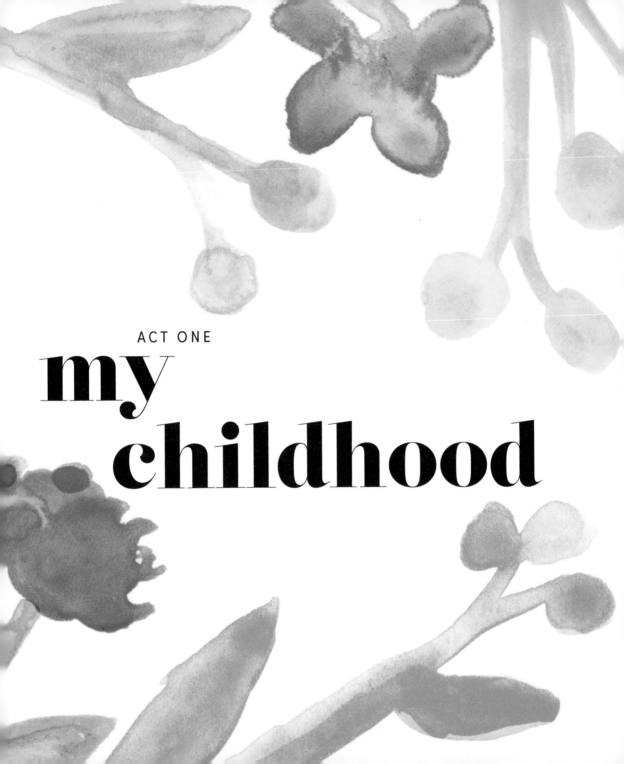

my childhood

about me

I WAS BORN ON:

_____

MY BIRTHPLACE IS:

_____

MY FULL NAME ON MY BIRTH CERTIFICATE:

_____

MY PARENTS CHOSE MY NAME BECAUSE:

_____

_____

_____

MY NICKNAME, WHO CHOSE IT, AND WHY:

_____

_____

_____

MY ASTROLOGICAL SIGN IS:

_____

HOW I RELATE TO MY SIGN:

_____

_____

_____

IN MY FAMILY, I WAS THE _____ ONE, BECAUSE:

_____

_____

_____

about my mother

MY MOTHER'S NAME:

_____

MY MOTHER'S LIFE DATES:

_____

HER BIRTHPLACE, WHERE SHE GREW UP, AND HER EDUCATION:

_____

_____

_____

_____

HER OCCUPATION(S)
before I was born and when I was growing up:

_____

_____

_____

THESE WORDS BEST DESCRIBE
MY MOTHER:

_____

_____

_____

THESE TRAITS ARE WHAT MAKE ME MY MOTHER'S DAUGHTER:

_____

_____

_____

HERE ARE SOME THINGS WE BONDED OVER:

_____

_____

_____

HER GREATEST ACCOMPLISHMENTS:

_____

_____

_____

THE MOST SIGNIFICANT LIFELONG VALUE MY MOTHER INSTILLED IN ME:

_____

_____

_____

about my father

MY FATHER'S NAME:

_____

MY FATHER'S LIFE DATES:

_____

HIS BIRTHPLACE, WHERE HE GREW UP, AND HIS EDUCATION:

_____

_____

_____

_____

HIS OCCUPATION(S)
before I was born and when I was growing up:

_____

_____

_____

THESE WORDS BEST DESCRIBE
MY FATHER:

_____

_____

_____

THESE TRAITS ARE WHAT MAKE ME MY FATHER'S DAUGHTER:

_____

_____

_____

HERE ARE SOME THINGS WE BONDED OVER:

_____

_____

_____

HIS GREATEST ACCOMPLISHMENTS:

_____

_____

_____

THE MOST IMPORTANT VALUE I LEARNED FROM MY FATHER WAS:

_____

_____

_____

my family

HERE'S THE STORY OF HOW MY PARENTS MET:

_____
_____
_____
_____
_____
_____
_____

AS A CHILD, I WOULD OBSERVE THEIR RELATIONSHIP.
It can best be described as:

_____
_____
_____
_____
_____
_____
_____
_____
_____

THE FAMILY MEMBERS (SIBLINGS, PETS, AND OTHERS)
living in our household included:

_____

_____

_____

_____

GROWING UP, I WAS ESPECIALLY CLOSE TO:

_____

_____

_____

_____

_____

_____

_____

Observing your relatives' attributes is like looking into a magic mirror.

my heritage

MY FAMILY ORIGINATED FROM:

_____

_____

_____

SOME INTERESTING STORIES ABOUT OUR FAMILY'S PAST:

_____

_____

_____

_____

_____

FAMILY HEIRLOOMS THAT I TREASURE ARE:

_____

_____

_____

my elders

MY GRANDPARENTS' NAMES, AND WHEN AND WHERE THEY WERE BORN:

_____

_____

_____

_____

THE ROLE THAT MY GRANDPARENTS PLAYED IN MY LIFE:

_____

_____

_____

_____

OTHER RELATIVES OR ADULTS WHO HAD A STRONG INFLUENCE ON ME:

_____

_____

_____

_____

ONE OF OUR BEST FAMILY GATHERINGS WAS:

_____

_____

_____

_____

_____

_____

_____

_____

_____

_____

_____

my early school years

SUPERLATIVES FOR MY DAYS IN ELEMENTARY SCHOOL

BEST FRIEND:

_____

BEST SCHOOL SUBJECT:

_____

FAVORITE TEACHER:

_____

FAVORITE BOOK:

_____

FAVORITE TELEVISION SHOW:

_____

BELOVED TOY:

_____

FAVORITE WEEKEND ACTIVITY:

_____

DREAM CAREER:

_____

FAVORITE SONG:

_____

FAVORITE OUTFIT: FAVORITE AFTER-SCHOOL ACTIVITY:

_____   _____

CHILDHOOD IDOL:

_____

MOST MEMORABLE NATIONAL/WORLD EVENT:

_____

BIGGEST CHORE/RESPONSIBILITY:

_____

AN INNOVATION THAT IMPACTED OUR LIVES:

_____

a little star

AT AN EARLY AGE, IT WAS EVIDENT THAT MY TALENT WAS:

_____

_____

_____

_____

AS A CHILD, I WAS MOST PASSIONATE ABOUT:

_____

_____

_____

_____

I RECEIVED AWARDS AND RECOGNITION FOR:

_____

_____

_____

_____

miss mischief!

OF COURSE, I WASN'T ALWAYS LITTLE MISS PERFECT!
Here's a story about a time I got in trouble, and what my parents did about it.

_____

_____

_____

_____

_____

_____

I CONFESS, SOMETIMES I GOT AWAY WITH MISCHIEF. HERE'S SUCH A TIME:

_____

_____

_____

_____

_____

_____

childhood challenges

WHEN I WAS LITTLE, MY BIGGEST FEAR WAS:

_____

_____

_____

_____

_____

_____

_____

HERE ARE SOME OF MY STRUGGLES,
how I solved them, and what I learned from them:

_____

_____

_____

_____

_____

_____

AS A FAMILY, THE MOST CHALLENGING TIME FOR US WAS WHEN:

_____

_____

_____

_____

_____

_____

_____

IF I COULD GIVE MY CHILDHOOD SELF SOME ADVICE NOW, I'D SAY:

_____

_____

_____

_____

_____

_____

_____

my teenage years

BEST FRIEND:

_____

BEST SCHOOL SUBJECT:

_____

FAVORITE TEACHER:

_____

FAVORITE BOOK:

_____

FAVORITE TELEVISION SHOW:

_____

FAVORITE MOVIE:

_____

FAVORITE WEEKEND ACTIVITY:

_____

DREAM CAREER:

_____

FAVORITE SONG:

_____

FAVORITE OUTFIT:

_____

EXTRACURRICULAR ACTIVITIES:

_____

TEEN IDOL:

_____

MOST MEMORABLE NATIONAL/WORLD EVENT:

_____

BIGGEST CHORE/RESPONSIBILITY:

_____

FIRST JOB:

_____

AN INNOVATION THAT IMPACTED OUR LIVES:

_____

take ten

A SNAPSHOT OF WHO I WAS AS A TEENAGER

1 THERE WAS ONE PERSON I KNEW
I COULD ALWAYS COUNT ON:

_____

_____

_____

2 THERE WERE SPECIFIC ITEMS OF CLOTHING
I'D WEAR ALL THE TIME. THEY WERE:

_____

_____

_____

3 THE MOST IMPORTANT LESSONS
I LEARNED IN HIGH SCHOOL WERE:

_____

_____

_____

4 I HAD SOME INSECURITIES.
THEY INCLUDED:

_____

_____

_____

5 THE PEOPLE WHO HAD A POSITIVE
EFFECT ON ME WERE:

_____

_____

_____

6 I FELT PROUD OF MY ACCOMPLISHMENTS, WHICH INCLUDED:

_____

_____

_____

7 SIGNIFICANT TRIPS THAT I TOOK:

_____

_____

_____

8 BOOKS, MOVIES, OR MUSIC THAT I REMEMBER LOVING:

_____

_____

_____

9 DURING MY SUMMER VACATIONS I'D:

_____

_____

_____

10 I CAN BEST DESCRIBE MYSELF AT THAT AGE WITH THESE THREE WORDS:

_____

_____

_____

young love

I HAD CRUSHES ON:

_____

_____

_____

_____

_____

I HAD SOME ADMIRERS. THEY WERE:

_____

_____

_____

_____

_____

DATING THEN WAS A LITTLE DIFFERENT THAN NOW.
This is how I remember my first date:

_____

_____

_____

_____

_____

_____

_____

HERE'S WHAT I CAN TELL YOU ABOUT MY FIRST LOVE
and other early relationships:

_____

_____

_____

_____

_____

_____

_____

_____

_____

_____

_____

teenage challenges

AS A TEENAGER, I WORRIED ABOUT DIFFERENT THINGS.
Some of those things included:

_____

_____

_____

_____

_____

MY RELATIONSHIP WITH MY PARENTS WAS:

_____

_____

_____

_____

_____

_____

IF I COULD GIVE MY TEENAGE SELF SOME ADVICE NOW, I'D SAY:

_____

_____

_____

_____

_____

_____

_____

_____

_____

_____

ACT TWO

woman–hood

take ten

A SNAPSHOT OF MY LIFE AS A YOUNG WOMAN

1 WHEN I LEFT HOME, THE FIRST PLACE I LIVED WAS:

_____
_____
_____

2 BEFORE MARRIAGE AND STARTING A FAMILY, IT WAS IMPORTANT TO ME THAT:

_____
_____
_____

3 I WANTED TO KEEP LEARNING, SO I:

_____
_____
_____

4 I REMEMBER SOME AWESOME TRIPS THAT I TOOK:

_____
_____
_____

5 THERE WAS A LOT GOING ON IN THE WORLD. I REMEMBER WHEN:

_____
_____
_____

6 SOME ACCOMPLISHMENTS THAT MADE ME PROUD WERE:

_____

_____

_____

7 THE PEOPLE I FELT ESPECIALLY CLOSE TO AT THE TIME WERE:

_____

_____

_____

8 BOOKS, MUSIC, OR MOVIES THAT I REMEMBER LOVING:

_____

_____

_____

9 WOMEN'S RIGHTS AND CAUSES CHANGED DURING MY LIFETIME. HERE'S HOW:

_____

_____

_____

10 THESE THREE WORDS BEST DESCRIBE ME AT THIS STAGE OF MY LIFE:

_____

_____

_____

monday to friday

MY EDUCATION CONTINUED
THROUGH:

_____
_____
_____
_____

MY RESPONSIBILITIES AS A YOUNG
WOMAN WERE:

_____
_____
_____
_____

THE WORK I DID WAS:

_____
_____
_____

A MAJOR MILESTONE IN MY WORK
WAS WHEN:

_____
_____
_____

ASIDE FROM MY WORK, I DREAMED
OF BECOMING:

_____
_____
_____

nights & weekends

IN MY DOWNTIME, HERE'S WHAT I DID TO RELAX:

_____

_____

_____

_____

_____

HOBBIES, CLUBS, OR VOLUNTEER WORK THAT I DEVOTED MYSELF TO:

_____

_____

_____

_____

AS A YOUNG WOMAN, I WAS ESPECIALLY INTERESTED IN AND FELT PASSIONATE ABOUT:

_____

_____

_____

falling in love

HERE'S WHAT MY DATING LIFE AND RELATIONSHIPS WERE LIKE
when I was a young woman:

_____

_____

_____

_____

_____

_____

_____

EVERYONE'S LOVE STORY IS UNIQUE. MY JOURNEY—
the one that eventually lead to grandmotherhood—began like this:

_____

_____

_____

_____

_____

_____

_____

WHEN I REFLECT ON ROMANCE,
I think about one particular time when:

_____

_____

_____

_____

_____

_____

_____

A FEW IMPORTANT THINGS THAT I'VE LEARNED
about love and relationships:

_____

_____

_____

_____

_____

_____

_____

starting a family

WHEN I LEARNED I WAS GOING TO BE A MOTHER, I FELT:

_____
_____
_____
_____
_____
_____
_____

WHAT WAS GOING ON IN THE WORLD AT THE TIME
affected my anticipation of motherhood because:

_____
_____
_____
_____

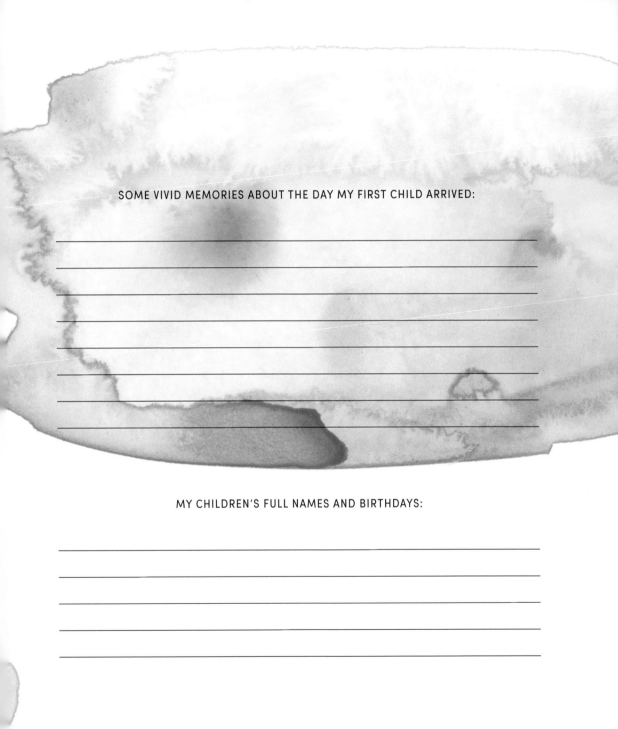

SOME VIVID MEMORIES ABOUT THE DAY MY FIRST CHILD ARRIVED:

_____

_____

_____

_____

_____

_____

_____

MY CHILDREN'S FULL NAMES AND BIRTHDAYS:

_____

_____

_____

_____

_____

new motherhood

MY STRONGEST MEMORIES OF EARLY MOTHERHOOD,
both wonderful and difficult, are:

_____

_____

_____

_____

_____

_____

THE PERSON (OR PEOPLE) WHO HELPED ME THE MOST:

_____

_____

_____

_____

_____

_____

I CHOSE TO ADOPT SOME OF MY PARENTS' WAYS WHEN IT CAME TO
raising my own family, such as:

_____

_____

_____

_____

_____

_____

_____

COMPARED TO MY UPBRINGING, THE THINGS I DID DIFFERENTLY WERE:

_____

_____

_____

_____

_____

_____

_____

_____

family dynamics

EVERYONE PLAYED A DIFFERENT ROLE IN OUR FAMILY

THE ONE TO MAKE THE RULES:

_____

THE ONE TO BREAK THE RULES:

_____

THE ONE WHO FOLLOWED THE RULES:

_____

THE BEST COOK:

_____

THE ONE EVERYONE WENT TO FOR ADVICE:

_____

THE ONE WHO WAS ALWAYS ON TIME:

_____

THE PERSON WHO WAS ALWAYS LATE:

_____

THE BEST STORYTELLER:

_____

THE PERSON WHO ALWAYS LISTENED BEST:

_____

THE MOST OPTIMISTIC ONE:

_____

THE MOST INDEPENDENT ONE:

_____

THE PERSON WITH EXCELLENT ORGANIZATIONAL SKILLS:

_____

THE ONE WHO WIPED AWAY THE TEARS:

_____

THE ONE WITH THE BEST SENSE OF HUMOR:

_____

THE MOST LEVELHEADED ONE:

_____

my family years

SUPERLATIVES FOR MY DAYS AS A MOTHER

OUR CLOSEST FAMILY FRIENDS:

_____

FAVORITE TEACHERS/COACHES:

_____

A FANTASTIC FAMILY TRIP:

_____

BOOKS WE LOVED READING TOGETHER:

_____

FAVORITE FAMILY TELEVISION SHOW:

_____

A GAME WE LOVED TO PLAY:

_____

FUN SLANG MY KID(S) TAUGHT ME:

_____

OUR FAVORITE WEEKEND ACTIVITY:

_____

FAVORITE FAMILY MEAL:

_____

FAVORITE FAMILY CONVERSATION TOPIC:

_____

FAVORITE HOLIDAY TRADITION:

_____

BEST PART OF SUMMER:

_____

A TOY MY KID(S) BEGGED FOR:

_____

AN INNOVATION THAT IMPACTED OUR LIVES:

_____

a mother's reflections

SOME ADDITIONAL OBSERVATIONS ABOUT MY OFFSPRING,
such as how I saw pieces of myself in them (and them in me), how we were different,
and what made me proud.

_____

_____

_____

_____

_____

_____

_____

_____

_____

_____

_____

_____

_____

_____

_____

_____

motherhood challenges

I WORRIED, AS MOTHERS DO. MOSTLY I WORRIED ABOUT:

_____

_____

_____

_____

_____

_____

I TRIED TO KEEP MY LIFE BALANCED BY:

_____

_____

_____

_____

_____

_____

_____

IF I HAD KNOWN THEN WHAT I KNOW NOW, I WOULD HAVE:

_____

_____

_____

_____

_____

_____

_____

_____

_____

_____

_____

_____

_____

_____

_____

_____

_____

Do not
let the fear
of the
unknown
engulf you.
Embrace
yourself.
Dare to live.

turning points

HERE ARE SOME OF THE BIGGEST CHALLENGES THAT I FACED IN MY ADULT LIFE,
and how I worked through them.

_____

_____

_____

_____

_____

_____

_____

_____

_____

_____

_____

_____

_____

_____

_____

_____

the grandest time

about
my grandchildren

HERE'S WHEN AND HOW I HEARD I WAS GOING TO BE A GRANDMOTHER, AND HOW I REACTED:

_____

_____

_____

_____

_____

_____

_____

_____

THE NAME I WANTED MY GRANDCHILDREN TO CALL ME WAS _____ BECAUSE:

_____

_____

_____

_____

_____

_____

_____

_____

WHEN I SAW MY FIRST GRANDCHILD, I FELT:

_____

_____

_____

_____

_____

_____

_____

_____

THE NAMES OF MY GRANDCHILDREN AND THEIR BIRTHDAYS:

_____

_____

_____

_____

_____

_____

From generation to generation, our values are the thread that holds us together.

generation next

WHEN MY CHILDREN BECAME PARENTS, I FELT:

_____

_____

_____

_____

HERE'S HOW WE STAY CONNECTED AND PARTICIPATE IN EACH OTHER'S LIVES:

_____

_____

_____

_____

I TRY TO CARRY OUT THESE TRADITIONS WITH MY GRANDCHILDREN:

_____

_____

_____

_____

my grand years

SUPERLATIVES FOR MY DAYS AS A GRANDMOTHER

A FANTASTIC FAMILY TRIP:

_____

A BOOK WE'VE READ TOGETHER:

_____

A MOVIE OR SHOW WE'VE WATCHED TOGETHER:

_____

A GAME WE LOVE TO PLAY:

_____

NEW SLANG MY GRANDKID(S) TAUGHT ME:

_____

MY FAVORITE WAY TO SPOIL THEM:

_____

A TOY THEY'VE BEGGED FOR:

_____

A MEAL THAT I MAKE JUST FOR THEM:

_____

FAVORITE HOLIDAY TRADITION:

_____

THE BEST PART OF SUMMER:

_____

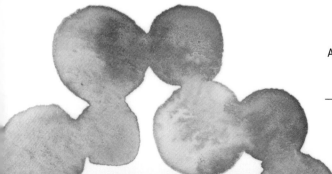

AN INNOVATION THAT IMPACTED OUR LIVES:

_____

quotable kids

SOME ADORABLE, HILARIOUS, AND PROFOUND WORDS
spoken by my grandchild(ren):

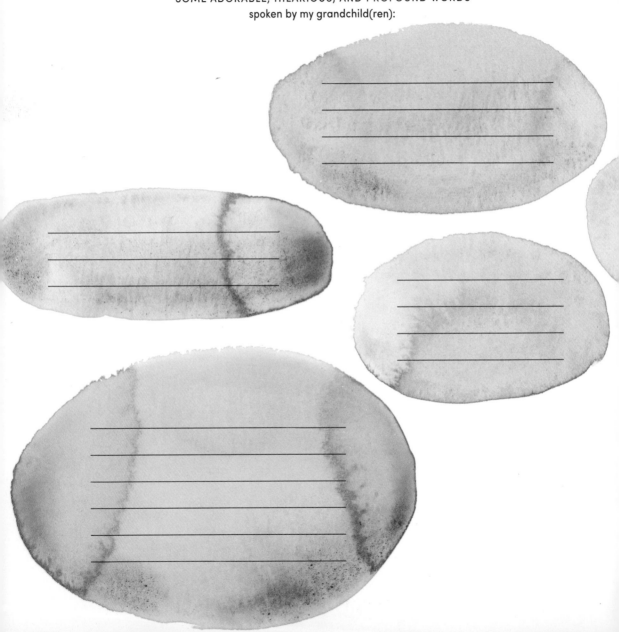

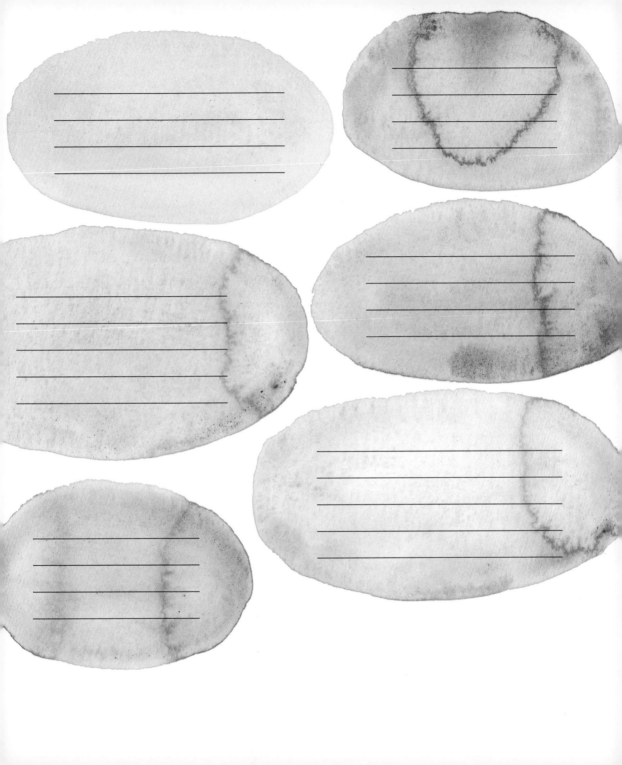

a grandmother's reflections

MEMORIES OF MY GRANDCHILDREN GROWING UP ARE ETCHED FOREVER IN MY MIND.
I am so proud of them because:

_____

_____

_____

_____

_____

_____

_____

_____

_____

_____

_____

_____

_____

_____

_____

_____

ACT FOUR

my
legacy

take ten

A SNAPSHOT OF ME TODAY

1 SOMEONE I CAN ALWAYS COUNT ON IS:

_____
_____
_____

2 I HAVE A TRUSTED DAILY ROUTINE. I ENJOY:

_____
_____
_____

3 IF I COULD HAVE THREE HISTORICAL FIGURES OVER FOR DINNER, THEY'D BE:

_____
_____
_____

4 I'LL ALWAYS REMEMBER THOSE IN MY LIFE WHO'VE INSPIRED ME. THEY ARE:

_____
_____
_____

5 MY FAVORITE PIECES OF CLOTHING ARE:

_____
_____
_____

6 IF I KNEW THAT I WAS ABOUT TO EAT
MY LAST MEAL, I'D ASK FOR:

_____
_____
_____

7 IF I'M FEELING BLUE, I CHEER MYSELF
UP BY:

_____
_____
_____

8 MY FAVORITE COLOR AND
SCENT ARE:

_____
_____
_____

9 A BOOK, FILM, OR WORK OF ART
THAT I ENJOYED RECENTLY WAS:

_____
_____
_____

10 GRATITUDE IS SO IMPORTANT
TO HAPPINESS. I AM GRATEFUL FOR:

_____
_____
_____

feeling good

SOME OF MY RECENT ACCOMPLISHMENTS ARE:

_____

_____

A DREAM I'M STILL REACHING FOR IS:

_____

_____

I'VE GROWN IN SO MANY WONDERFUL WAYS.
Since my younger years I've become more:

_____

_____

A QUALITY I WOULD LIKE TO WORK ON IS:

_____

_____

BASED ON MY EXPERIENCES,
I really hope you'll find time to visit these places:

_____

_____

FEARS I LEARNED TO OVERCOME INCLUDE:

_____

_____

I STILL HAVE ONE FEAR, AND THAT IS:

_____

_____

FROM A WORLDLY PERSPECTIVE, SOME THINGS NEVER CHANGE, SUCH AS:

_____

_____

my roots

GRANDPARENTS

_____

_____

PARENTS

_____

ME

_____

_____

_____

_____

GREAT-GRANDPARENTS

_____

_____

_____

_____

_____

_____

_____

_____

GREAT-GREAT-GRANDPARENTS

_____

_____

_____

_____

_____

_____

_____

_____

_____

_____

_____

_____

_____

my branches

ME / MY SPOUSE(S)

OUR CHILDREN

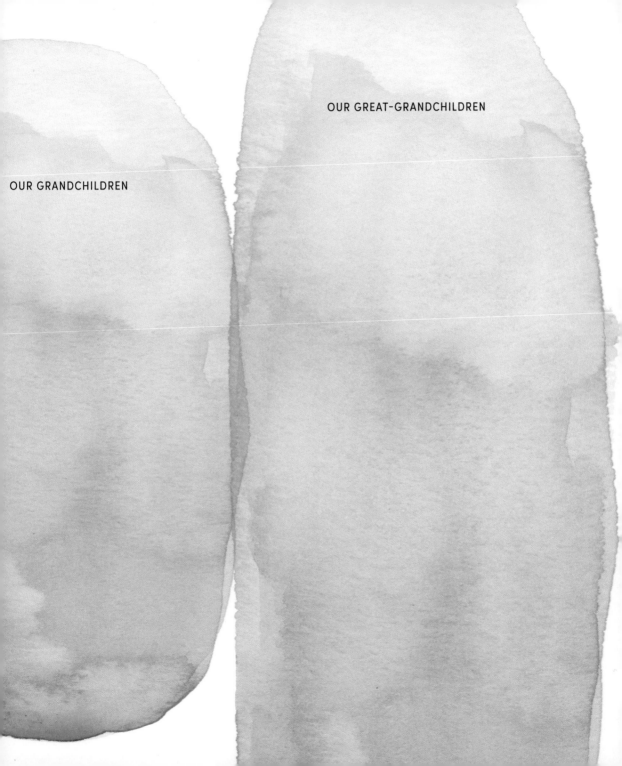

OUR GREAT-GRANDCHILDREN

OUR GRANDCHILDREN

Take a, big bite out of life.

my closing thoughts

I'M SO GRATEFUL TO BE YOUR GRANDMOTHER.
Here's what I've learned from you:

_____

_____

_____

_____

_____

_____

_____

_____

_____

_____

_____

_____

ALL MY LOVE,

_____

photos & memories

I want to acknowledge my husband, Sheldon Good,
my parents, Elaine and Roy Lang, and my honey bees
at HoneyGood.com–Susan Berman Hammer, Carolyn Jones,
and Ines Grzeslo–for their love and confidence in me.

To share your photos and memories, visit HoneyGood.com.

Design, Illustrations, and Cover Art by Isabel Urbina Peña

ISBN: 978-1-4197-3472-4

Text © 2019 Gramma Good LLC
Illustrations and Cover Art © 2019 Abrams

Printed and bound in China
10 9 8 7 6 5 4 3 2 1

Abrams Noterie products are available at special discounts when purchased
in quantity for premiums and promotions as well as fundraising or educational
use. Special editions can also be created to specification. For details, contact
specialsales@abramsbooks.com or the address below.

Abrams Noterie® is a registered trademark of Harry N. Abrams, Inc.

ABRAMS The Art of Books
195 Broadway, New York, NY 10007
abramsbooks.com